YOUR KNOWLEDGE HAS VALUE

- We will publish your bachelor's and
  master's thesis, essays and papers

- Your own eBook and book -
  sold worldwide in all relevant shops

- Earn money with each sale

Upload your text at www.GRIN.com
and publish for free

Mareike Hümmerich

Particpiation in nursing praxis and sciences

GRIN Publishing

Bibliographic information published by the German National Library:

The German National Library lists this publication in the National Bibliography; detailed bibliographic data are available on the Internet at http://dnb.dnb.de .

Imprint:

Copyright © 2008 GRIN Verlag GmbH
Print and binding: Books on Demand GmbH, Norderstedt Germany
ISBN: 978-3-640-74105-2

This book at GRIN:

http://www.grin.com/en/e-book/158186/particpiation-in-nursing-praxis-and-sciences

GRIN - Your knowledge has value

Since its foundation in 1998, GRIN has specialized in publishing academic texts by students, college teachers and other academics as e-book and printed book. The website www.grin.com is an ideal platform for presenting term papers, final papers, scientific essays, dissertations and specialist books.

Visit us on the internet:

http://www.grin.com/

http://www.facebook.com/grincom

http://www.twitter.com/grin_com

Katholische Fachhochschule NRW – Abteilung Köln, Fachbereich
Gesundheitswesen
Kooperatives Interdisziplinäres Seminar mit Videokonferenzen im Rahmen eines
deutsch-palästinensischen Austauschprojektes SS 2008

Dozent

Referat

Participation in german nursing practice and sciences

Partizipation in der Pflegepraxis und -wissenschaft

Mareike Hümmerich

Participation in German nursing

Preamble

„Participation" is no usual, conversational term in the German nursing language. Translated as "part taking" and "co-determination" participation means the political co-determination of the public in bills and in democratic elections. If the German nursing literature and language speaks of participation we rather use terms like "patient self-government" and "self-determination" which mean cooperation or participation in nursing and caring processes.

Saunders (1995) who explicitly uses the term of patient participation defines it as „active process of participation in and advancement of therapeutic or general self nursing abilities or the participiation in decisions concerning from reception to dismissal"[1]

My presentation follows the central Theme "Participiation" in this way of definition.

I will give you an overview about the concepts of Participation in the vocational training of nurses, in nursing sciences and especially in the practice of nursing. Therefore i give you an outline of the different areas.

1. Participations in the educational laws of nursing profession

In 2003 the training of nurses was based on new educational laws.

With the withdrawal from bio-medical concepts of focussing only on illness and instead putting the focus on health salutogenetic views and focussing on abilities become highly important in training. The motivating question in nursing is no longer "What makes you ill?" but "What keeps you healthy?" and by this consequently includes the clients right of self determination and self nursing abilities.

Accordingly our educational aim is as follows:

"According to the generally accepted degree of knowledge in nursing sciences, medical and other sciences…the education of nurses …is supposed to teach specialized, personal, social and methodical competences for responsible cooperation in healing, discovering and preventing diseases. Nursing is to focus on the restoration, the improvement, the preservation and the advancement of the physical and psychological health of the client by including preventive, rehabilitative and palliative measures.

In doing this the diverse nursing and living situations as well as the living phases and the independence and self determination of the clients have to be considered."(vgl. GROSSKOPF 2007)

---

[1] (BRÜGGEMANN S.73)

2. Participation in nursing sciences and research

Though nursing sciences and research is a rather young branch of science pretentious standards of self determination, autonomy and self nursing are evident in its theories, concepts and results of research. Several theories and studies often adopted from the Anglo-American are based on these central ideas.

For example the american nursing scientist Dorothy E. Orem, obliged to the principle of subsidiary as a principle of Christian social science, speaks of the standards of „self-care" and „dependent-care". The latter meaning the care thorugh relatives.

Only if both systems – the system of self-care and the system of dependent -care (care through relatives, neighbours, friends) is not sufficient to fulfil the requirements of care, professional nursing-care is justified.

The principle of participation is also reflected in the various nursing practises (nursing practice systems) that are carried out in cooperation with the client and/or his relatives depending on the degree of decision making abilities and competency (partial-compensatory or supportive-educating nursing practice system).

According to Orem the complete overtaking of nursing (complete compensatory nursing practice system) by a professional nurse is only justified in exceptions and usually in a temporally very restricted way.

Most nursing theories and concepts work with the so called nursing process meaning a working method that structures the complexe nursing practice comprehending several systematically combined phases:

→ assessment of the situation and of the requirements of nursing
→ setting of nursing aims and measures of nursing
→ the actual nursing
→ its evaluation.

Hereby the process of nursing is understood as a process of solving problems and a process of relation that is jointly shaped throughout all phases by both parties - the professionals and the client with his relatives.

Although if a client is able and willing to consume such an active self determining role it depends among other things on the kind and development of his desease.

A study of I.Brüggemann using the example of chronically diseased dialysis patients shows that especially chronically diseased assumes a passive patient's role.

The restrictions and dependencies of dialysis go together with strong physical and particularly with psychological burdens.

The life of the afflicted person depends on the dialysis. That means he permanently threatened by death.

„These aspects and a complex regime of treatment have consequences for the concept of life. The conception of the patient about how to organize the course depends on biography, duration of illness, symptoms of the disease, knowledge, experience and conviction as well as his relationship to doctors, nurses and relatives.“[2]

This passivity is confirmed by another study done in GB in which a client describes his own attitude as follows:

„„I prefer that my doctor makes the final decision about which treatment will be used, but seriously considers my opinion (zit. n. Caress, 1996 46)““[3]

Again another study by Biley shows that a client can only participate under the following circumstances:

- summary of physical wellness/fitness
- knowledge/information
- organization of the hospital

Wellness and physical fitness depend on the degree of recovery, kind of disease, progress of disease and other things. Here nursing has the opportunity to be influential and to enhance physical well being through diverse therapeutical and communicative concepts.

3. Participation in the context of social politics, rights and institution

The rights of patients can be derived from the Foundational Law of Germany. The first article says: „The dignity of man is inviolable. To respect and protect it is the duty of all national power. “[4]

In Germany people take their own person, their needs and their rights very serious. But to make use of their right of co-determination and co-decision they need a pool of information.

„Concerning the status of a patient „the German jurisdiction developed the following principle: not the wellbeing of the patient is of first importance but the will of the patient is decisive““ (vgl. Schell 1998)[5]

Therefore the following patient's rights can be concluded for health care:

1. The right of man
2. The right of Information
3. The right of consent
4. The right of privacy
5. The right of nursing and treatment

---

[2] (BRÜGGEMANN S.37)

[3] (BRÜGGEMANN S.39)

[4] (Bundestag S.7)

[5] (JUCHLI 2004 S.115)

(vgl. JUCHLI 2004, S. 116)

Possibilities for patients to assume their right of self determination are:

- authority of provision
- decree of care
- Living will

Authority of provision

In this way a person can determine who will take over decisions and business in case of legal incapacity before he is needing care.

He can give the person of his choice authority. Such an authority of provision should exactly define the case of provision and should for evidence sake be put down in written form. To prevent all doubts concerning its authenticity a notary attestation is recommended.

Decree of care

Giving authority is different from a decree of care. If a sufficient authorization has been given a decree of care is not possible. But everyone is allowed to determine which person should take care of him in case of needing care. (vgl. GROSSKOPF/KLEIN 2007)

Testament of patient

"The testament of patient or „living will" is an assignment in which the patient still legally capable describes the conditions under which treatments should be carried out or omitted."[6]

4. Participation in organisation

One way of organization in hospitals is the concept of briefing at the patients' bed. This concept has spread in the practice of nursing over the last years. I want to quickly outline it. Up to now the briefing took place at the ward using the patient files. The briefing with the patient takes place in the patients room.Of course the privacy and data protection have to be considered.

„ The briefing with the patient is a report of one shift to the following participating the nursing persons and the patient. Together with the patient current nursing aspects and measures are discussed."[7]

The goal is the objective and relevant passing on of information to nursing colleagues. On the other hand this procedure enhances transparency. The patient always has the opportunity to ask questions and to clarify obscurities. In this way he actively takes part in the process of nursing and therapy planning.

---

[6] (GROSSKOPF 2007 S.153)

[7] (JUCHLI 2004 S.162}

The nurses are expected to communicate in clear, simple language and to act and react professionally. In this way the patient is included, receives information and is therby able to make decisions. (vgl. THIEME 2004 S.162; RENNEN-ALTHOFF 200 S.605)
In case further advice is necessary it can be given after the briefing or at a later suitable time.

Conclusion
The different manifestations of participation, of the patients' part in the nursing events can only exemplarily be represented.

1. The term participation is not common in Germany. Participation is usually used in politics. In nursing the term means an „active process of participation in therapeutic or general self care abilities or the participation in decision making processes concerning the patients reception, dismissal and everything in between."

2. The preservation of self caring abilities is the declared educational aim of the German Health nursing training. „Nursing is to focus on the restoration, the improvement, the preservation and the advancement of the physical and psychological health of the client by including preventive, rehabilitative and palliative measures.   In doing this the diverse nursing and living situations as well as the living phases and the independence and self determination of the clients have to be considered. (vgl. GROSSKOPF 2007)

3. In her theory of self care the nursing scientist Orem emphasizes the independence. The self determination of the client is to be considered according to the principle of subsidarity. As different studies show the willingness of partaking in decision processes is influenced by the kind and duration of the disease and different other factors.

4. The patient's rights can be derived from the foundational law of Germany. The German jurisdiction developed the following principle: „not the well being of the patient is of first importance but the will of the patient is decisive." This principle is visible in the already mentioned concepts (Mrs. Orem) , functions (decree of care and patients testament) and structures (briefing at the patients bed).

Literaturverzeichnis:

2003. *The ICN Definition of Nursing.* Available at: <http://www.icn.ch/definition.htm>
[Accessed at 13 March 2008].

BUNDESTAG, D. *Deutscher Bundestag: I. Die Grundrechte.* Deutscher Bundestag. Available
at: <http://www.bundestag.de/parlament/funktion/gesetze/grundgesetz/gg_01.html>
[Accessed at 14 March 2008].

BRÜGGEMANN, I. Patientenpartizipation im Krankenhaus - Anspruch und Wirklichkeit am
Beispiel von Dialyspatienten. *Printernet,* 2006 (01), 36–52.

FAWCETT, J., 1996. *Pflegemodelle im Überblick.* Bern: Huber.

GROßKOPF, V., 2007. *Vorschriften und Gesetze für das Gesundheitswesen.* Balingen:
Spitta. (Spitta Fachbuchreihe Medizin).

GROßKOPF, V. and KLEIN, H., 2007. *Recht in Medizin und Pflege.* 3., vollst. überarb. und
aktualisierte Aufl. Balingen: Spitta-Verl.

HUNDENBORN, G., 2007. *Fallorientierte Didaktik in der Pflege. Grundlagen und Beispiele
für Ausbildung und Prüfung.* München: Elsevier Urban & Fischer.

JUCHLI, L. et al., 2004. *Thiemes Pflege. Professionalität erleben ; 219 Tabellen ; [mit 75
Filmen auf 4 CDs!].* 10., völlig neu bearb. Aufl. Stuttgart: Thieme.

OELKE, U., HUNDENBORN, G. and KÜHN, C., eds., November 2003. *Richtlinie für die
Ausbildung in der Gesundheits- und Krankenpflege sowie in der Gesundheitsund
Kinderkrankenpflege. Im Auftrag des Ministeriums für Gesundheit, Soziales, Frauen und
Familie des Landes Nordrhein-Westfalen.* Deutsches Institut für angewandte
Pflegeforschung. Köln.

RENNEN-ALLHOFF, B. and SCHAEFFER, D., 2000. *Handbuch Pflegewissenschaft.*
Weinheim: Juventa-Verl.

SCHUBERT, K. Klein, 2006. *Das Politiklexikon.*

WIESMANN, U. Universität Greifswald and SCHULZ, J. Humboldt-Universität Berlin, 2007.
Der Mensch als biopsychosoziale Einheit. Universität Greifswald.